WHA

love
Sianna
Catrancu

ESSENTIAL POETS SERIES 133

Canada Council   Conseil des Arts
for the Arts   du Canada

ONTARIO ARTS COUNCIL
CONSEIL DES ARTS DE L'ONTARIO

Guernica Editions Inc. acknowledges the support
of The Canada Council for the Arts.
Guernica Editions Inc. acknowledges the support
of the Ontario Arts Council.

GIANNA PATRIARCA

WHAT MY ARMS CAN CARRY

GUERNICA
TORONTO – BUFFALO – CHICAGO – LANCASTER (U.K.)
2005

Antonio D'Alfonso, editor
Guernica Editions Inc.
P.O. Box 117, Station P, Toronto (ON), Canada M5S 2S6
2250 Military Road, Tonawanda, N.Y. 14150-6000 U.S.A.

Distributors:
University of Toronto Press Distribution,
5201 Dufferin Street, Toronto, (ON), Canada M3H 5T8

Gazelle Book Services, White Cross Mills, High Town
Lancaster LA1 1XS U.K.

Independent Publishers Group,
814 N. Franklin Street, Chicago, Il. 60610 U.S.A.

Typesetting by Selina.
First edition.
Printed in Canada.

Legal Deposit — Third Quarter
National Library of Canada
Library of Congress Catalog Card Number: 2005921438
Library and Archives Canada Cataloguing in Publication
Patriarca, Gianna
What my arms can carry / Gianna Patriarca.
(Essential poets series ; 133)
ISBN 1-55071-211-X
I. Title. II. Series.
PS8581.A6665W43   2005   C811'.54   C2005-900846-6

Contents

These poems are for my cousins
Maria Grazia and Liliana Nalli,
because your hearts live with me in Toronto
and mine lives with you in Ceprano.
In memory of my cousin Linda
and for all women who have suffered violence.

Acknowledgements

I want to thank my publisher Antonio D'Alfonso and Guernica Editions for their continued support. A sincere thank you to the Ontario Arts Council, to my friends and family who inspire me and a special thank you to my husband Andrew for his patience and love. Some of these poems appeared in a limited short collection entitled *The Invisible Woman,* by LyricalMyrical. Thank you to Luciano Iacobelli. "The Neighbourhood Is Changing" was published in the magazine *Accenti* in 2002.

A tutti i miei amici in Italia, grazie per i ricordi, le risate, la storia.

You must grieve for this right now,
you have to feel this sorrow now,
for the world must be loved this much
if you're going to say "I lived" . . .
                              Nazim Hikmet

Dance with me . . . dance with me . . .
we are the song . . . we are the music . . .
Dance with me . . .
                              Nikki Giovanni

The call of memory no longer makes
me sad.
I have no complaints about
memories.
In fact, I have no complaints
about anything,
not even my heart
          aching nonstop like a big tooth.
                              Nazim Hikmet

What My Arms Can Carry

how do i package
the weight of my heart

i will take with me
what my arms can carry

a suitcase
a handful of photographs
the cotton shawls
my grandmother crocheted
with the dimming light
of her dark blue eyes

i will take with me
my grandfather's watch
on the silver chain
the carved wooden handle
of his bent cane
these things
i will honour
in a special place
in my new home

these things will remind me
of who i am
and where i came from

but who i am is many things

i am a name and a landscape
a language and a dialect
i am memory and history

the present and the future
i am the children i will bear
the man and woman
who will survive

i will take with me
what my arms can carry

Street of Widows

For Mamma

they live alone
in their own house
paid for
free of mortgage
they will not leave quietly
for anyone's convenience
not their own children
not their children-in-law

they will be carried out
one or two will fall victim
to the disintegration
of muscle and bone
the others will be victims
of time

but for now
it is their street
the street of widows
where my mother lives
where she visits the others
whose husbands are more
recent losses

they prepare tables
with crisp cotton tablecloths
fill them with all the talent
from their individual hands
they feed each other
stories and food

the occasional glass of red wine
then they laugh till sleep comes

they are strong with each other
understand everything without
extra words
they connect arms
into an unbreakable chain
and take evening walks
to the local church
where God waits
a little reluctant
and then
an ice cream
on their way home

My Mother Wants

my mother is a practical woman
she wants nothing more
than my complete happiness

nothing more than to hear
my voice each day
free of anxiety or pain

nothing more than to know
my heart is strong and
full of love

she births me again
with every heartbeat
it is this unbelievable need
to love me with every molecule
that keeps her breathing

she needs nothing more
than my dreams, my ambitions
to know success

my mother wants only my truth
never acknowledging the lies
between us they are non-existent

i am completely at home
in her love

there is no country or flag
no discourse on belonging
that must allow birth a definition

it is pure love that makes it home
i too am a practical woman
i want nothing more than
my mother to live
forever

The Neighbourhood Is Changing

the old men
have nowhere to go
banished, corroded barges
in some abandoned port
they sit
cooled by the winds of
passing streetcars
at the corner of Grace Street
and College

the faded wooden benches
are the only welcoming seats
that accommodate their time
so much time now
since their backs gave out
and their legs have jelly in them
since the pool halls became cafés
some see the world clearly
others through the pearly veils
of fallen cataracts
but their conversations are loud
and lucid
still the passion in their voices
in the stories they pitch
to each other
in the need to be heard

the old men sit
and the old women walk
the length of Grace Street
to the grand doors of St. Francis
each morning at eight

the doors open to prayers
to the lighting of candles
the necessary confessions
the blessing of the Eucharist

i make my way
in the neighbourhood
school bag in hand
the old men tip their hats
and offer a greeting

buon giorno, signora
i have time for a smile
a few words about the weather
the impending arthritis
the change in the neighbourhood
then i am off
to the sound of a bell
to fill the needs of my students

i will see them again
on my way home
heavy with the day's stress
and obligations
they are still there
waiting for the sun
to retire

sometimes i am aware there is
one old man less
one less story to pitch
one less voice to greet my mornings
one less hat tipped to existence
sì, il quartiere sta' cambiando

Basements

when does life
begin to smell like death

when does a woman
become an old woman

this house i have come to visit
where an old woman lives
just a few short years
since the last summer i was here
this same house
my cousins and i trampled through
in the flash of decades
the record player blasting out
Buddy Holly, Dion and Presley
this old woman's basement
was our kingdom
of plastic and wood veneer
a castle with etched smoky mirrors
polyester prints over the windows
linoleum flowers faded by footprints
chrome chairs with plaid seats
tall ashtrays on portable stands
this altar to the 1960s
this den of bad taste
where life happened
is now empty

the kitchen table
the twelve mismatched chairs
still there
but nobody comes for dinner

i stand by the door
a draft of silence
at my shoulders
remembering the old woman
who stands by the stove
elements glowing
boiling, simmering, frying
the steamed windows
smells that were life

there is something different
in my nostrils
it is unpleasant
i cannot decipher the lie
the truth or the memory

there is a different smell
to the old woman
on the threshold of death

she is just a little afraid
a little reluctant to stretch
out her leg

i will open a window

Johnny's Street

In memory of Johnny Lombardi

for the elderly who stubbornly stroll down
the streets they built but do not own.
Antonio D'Alfonso

the old man walks measured steps
no longer the quick strides of a hungry
or driven man

the hand guides the cane for balance and rest
he knows the pavement well
has counted the footsteps for decades
from his front door to his empire

this street is home
it was home to his father before him
home to my father not long ago
before the bars and trendy cafés
before the long evening promenades

before it became cool
to be who we are

now we are the requested flavour
the desired trend
he can stroll arm in arm with
identity

there was a time
the men could not linger
had to keep moving
footsteps in search of doorways

in search of destinations
where the welcome was not suspect
the laughter not misunderstood
where the undecipherable tongue
became song and conversation
making tolerable
the exile

this ordinary, nothing street
stretching five city blocks
unassuming and humble
has altered the face of a city
because certain men risked the walk

time has done its job
the little grocery store is gone
no more the smell of fish market
no more the multitude of bushels
on sidewalks
beans and eggplants brilliant
beneath a more polite
September sun

there is little left here
my father would recognize
few who recall the struggle

but there is the old man
and the elegance of aging
the continuity of a young boy
who has inherited blood
he walks side by side
with his grandfather

there is a tenderness
a respect in what is passed on

this is Johnny's street
it was my father's street
it is my street
a gift of inheritance

it is the heartbeat of our fathers
reverberating
long after the bars
have closed

Missing

For my cousin Linda, murdered June 7, 2002

> *I mean, however and wherever we are,*
> *we must live as if one never dies.*
>
> Nazim Hikmet

her eyes are blue
like her grandmother's
blue eyes
like my grandmother's
the news reports always
get it wrong
not *all* Italian women
have brown eyes
Linda is missing
my mother is desperate
in her cries
her sister's granddaughter
disappeared
cancelled
erased
as easily as a pencil mark
by a penny rubber

a whole woman
deleted
on a sunny afternoon
in February
no blood
no traces of flesh

a middle-aged woman
lovely and real

this is not cyberspace
it is Richmond Hill
it is Yonge Street
and Major McKenzie
one kilometer from home
from her son's bed
her kitchen utensils
her potted geraniums

it is the fifteenth day
and they will not admit
perhaps there is *foul play*

still the tedious investigation
the routines
the silence
the days

another case
just another case in this
city that moves like a shark
indiscriminate of prey

that you are Linda
means nothing at all
that you are a treasured pearl
on a string of beads
that extends for centuries
on your mother's side
on your father's side

it means nothing at all
that the officer said
you weren't *urgent* enough

to warrant a *warrant*

is all that matters

*

i was my mother's child
with ringlet curls and blue eyes
i was my father's little girl
my brother's playmate
my grandparent's pride and joy
this was only the beginning

i learned to walk
stumbling along the way
curious of the world and life
i was a young girl who danced
i had a first love
my heart was once broken
this was only the beginning

i grew to be a woman and dared to dream
i worked to make some dreams come true
i wore a white dress covered in lace
i gave my heart again to love
love gave me a son
this was only the beginning

i did not choose to leave willingly
i was not prepared
life sometimes chooses for you
and i was left simply to confront
this is the heartbreaking truth
my message is simple and sincere

i was with you in love
and it is in love that i leave you
remember me not in sadness
not in anger or revenge
because these are not joyous words

i am with you always in love
and love is
the beginning

*

i am my mother's child
i have inherited her shape
her colour
i have the same hands
but i have grown much taller

i am my mother's child
i walk with careful steps
but my feet are much larger

and less secure

i do not know
where the path will lead me
her street is well established

i know only that i am
my mother's child
her female child who
resembles a grandmother
a great aunt, a distant cousin
what woman was my grandmother

what woman is my mother
what woman am i

elegant and beautiful as the photograph
suggests
troubled or happy
lonely or alone

am i each of these women
at moments of my life
i am all of these women
each day of my life

blundering along
entering and exiting doorways
each offering assurance
each a possibility

there are sisters i meet
along the way
balancing something unique
i hold out my hand
together our steps advance

i am my mother's child
i am a mother to my child
i am a woman who stumbles
and sometimes
falls

Woman Behind the Wall

punish me with death
all sins, all mistakes
all rights and wrongs
into the same dark hole

i am the woman
disappeared with her sins
and her glories
four months behind a wall
while my son cried himself to sleep
my mother prayed herself into limbo

punish me again
for trusting
for falling in and out of love
for falling into a mistake

withdraw me in silence
erase me quickly
because you are sure
that i have sinned

what do you know about sin
about my sins
as weak as we are
less than our dreams
living always in the warmth
the greenhouse of needs

a woman made flesh
a woman trusting her heart
i am here behind a wall
punish me

Mothers and Breasts

Trees are never felled . . . in summer . . .
Not when the fruit . . . is yet to be borne
Nikki Giovanni

all too suddenly
my baby
has developed breasts

young woman's breasts

all too suddenly
there is the obsession
of breasts

the shape
the size
the need for the perfect bra
the exact colour
the exclusive material
the comparison
the competition
the design beneath the t-shirt
the desired illusion
in the three-way mirror

at fourteen
there is the need to hide
everything from me

the nipples behind the towel
the distance of her desires
the whispered words
don't look, mom

as if i had no breasts of my own
as if i had never seen
her tender body
scrubbed her clean
powdered every centimeter
of who she is
held her warm and fragrant
in my arms

my baby pushes away
the need for me
with such delicacy
and precision

hiding her belly button
her spindly legs
too long to have yet
developed shape
her angel face
too young to bear history
too sweet to begin
tasting the bitterness of
time

i remember my fourteenth year
differently
wanting my mother desperately
wanting the questions
the interest
wanting answers and more

my mother was too tired
too catholic
too sad
to recognize my needs

i vowed to be different
it is not always about choice
not always about what is correct
not always the right time

perhaps when she is fifteen
perhaps when i am fifty-one

Our Worlds

each day she pushes me
a little further away

my world shrinking
hers fattening

i didn't think it would
happen so fast

i have circled the planet
leaving her footprints

she has bought her first
high heeled shoes

i wanted our world
to last a little longer

Nostalgia

if i dare to write
about the evenings
on the front porch
on the wooden verandah
the thousand and one
evenings or more
that were our youth
i am accused of writing
nostalgia

as if the word
was somehow
sinful
as if the tears inspired
by the beauty of a full moon
on an August night
were fraudulent

as if the stars
were only science
and held no other
history

as if the walnut tree
we used to climb
was just a tree

as if poetry
no longer lived
on any page
words replaced by
performance

but i will remember
the porch
i will remember
the moon and the stars
that semi-brick house
on a nothing street
in this nothing city
where our parents
made a home
where we dreamed
and counted stars
like accumulated lovers
drank cherry cokes
and let Dusty Springfield
sing our hearts

we had no car
to liberate us
no money in our pockets
no man to take us away
nothing but the porch
and the evening sky
and a lifetime
to commit our sins

take me home
i want to remember
the streets we played in
without the memory
there is only
anger

The Winter I Was Ten

the winter i was ten
snow attempted to
swallow the city

my first Canadian winter
in the shaky house by the
railroad tracks

the dead end street
where Henry's father
had dumped his Ford pick-up
with the four flat tires
and broken headlights

it was the winter
our faces froze to the windowpanes
imagining the North Pole

my mother
young and new
apprehensive
to free us into this unknown
white world

it was the winter
the cardboard box became
a sled
my sister light and fearless
sat inside
her bold little heart
her inquisitive eyes
ready for any adventure

my cheeks fleshy, ripe and red
as mamma's lipstick

up and down the dead end street
until the box completely melted
into the snow
leaving only brown shreds
chocolate stains on a
pristine tablecloth

the winter i was ten
the snow was mystical
the world was white
the winter lasted longer
than a lifetime

The Anniversary, Nov. 16

eighteen years, papa
and it is yesterday

it is only today
all days are one memory

all years memory
softening

there are flowers
rooted to the earth
a handful of tables
outside our favourite café
this November is spilling
with unusual sunshine

your last day was much colder
dusted with the first snow
colours hidden
the world wanting an early nap

tonight after visiting you
i am alone
a rare thing these days
the job
the children
the house
the husband
the poems
    mamma

you cannot believe
how much of me i share
did you know me well, papa
did you hide it carefully

i am sitting at the last
table of two
by the window
looking out at the intersection
of Clinton and College
you knew this corner well

i'm drinking a glass of wine
instead of coffee
New Zealand Sauvignon Blanc
how sophisticated
i have become

always a pen in hand
ready to speak to silence
the way i now speak to you
not needing presence
of flesh or friend

i can sit alone
i can order a meal
i can order wine
without feeling embarrassed
without being a woman
alone

i am all grown up, papa
i can be me
all by myself

i can talk to you
without anger

you would be proud

Saint Joseph

did my father
ever hold me in his arms
with so much love
with so much patience

how gentle you are
as you hold your woman's child
Joseph with the white lily
and the pure heart
with the trim brown beard
and timid smile
patron saint of families
father of all fathers
carpenter and man

silent Joseph
no words
ever spoken
only your presence
strong and secure

my eyes will not move from you
in this church
where you stand dry and cold
in the darkest corner
barren of sunlight
only the dim flicker of an electric
candle

is it this church that inspires
me to cry
this church where my father

stood next to me
my little girl's body
in a communion dress
of pure white polyester
my head adorned with lace and
plastic pearls
my father had no lily
he had no beard
an ordinary man
in a gray suit
a thin blue tie
my father and me
his arms stiff against his chest
my bride's dress starched against
my nervous knees

was he proud of me, Joseph
as you are proud
of your woman's child

Franky's Girl

we all wanted a daddy
like Nancy had

Nancy with the laughing face
and Frank's celebrated arms
around her

lovely Nancy in dancing dresses
and miniature pearls

lucky Nancy with pony rides
on birthdays
and endless merry-go-rounds

we all wanted a daddy
who sang us love songs

a daddy who placed warm kisses
on our waiting cheeks

a daddy who wasn't afraid
to show the world a daughter

and gush with pride

Dundas and Sackville

i don't come down to this part of town much anymore
not that i ever did before
we all had our own ghettos
we felt comfortable in
we had our own corners of the city
where faces recognized each other
and lessened the fear

this evening my teenage daughter is painting children's
    faces
in the church hall of St. Cyril
a community celebration before Christmas
my child is volunteering her time for a school project
and i have driven her here
where we will probably
not come again
so far from our lives

the hall is noisy with children of every shape
of every colour
their laughter unites them
laughter has no country

popcorn machines, hot dogs and candy floss
grown-ups dressed in fantasy costumes
Mickey Mouse and Spiderman

the mothers sit on rows of fold-out chairs
their faces tired and beautiful
some are oblivious to it all but others wear their
fatigue like an old dress
the air is scented with needs

maybe i have worn the wrong clothes
i once believed it was my height and my weight
that invited the stares
there are women here
larger than i will ever be
it is
something different they recognize
not the leather gloves or the silk scarf
it is about belonging
it is about crossing lines

it was not very long ago
an immigrant child
ran around the great hall of St. Francis
where my mother sat with other women
tired and distant
the dust of factories and basements in their eyes

The Cuba Poem

What new rhythm will I discover today
Rinaldo Arenas

how beautiful
how sad

this island of sun and sea
of rhythm and revolution
this island free of America
except for the green green dollar
and the blue blue jeans
craving the Nike emblem
and Mickey Mouse dream

this island
Arenas dared to love
forbidden loves
where his heart attempted
escape
only the words were ever
free

*

i am a small bourgeois
a pale dreamer
from a Canadian season
come to bury
my aches in the white sand
to darken my skin
awaken my tongue
with healing salt

i come with the romance of Che
in my assailable heart
the urgency to equalize life
believing passion is all it takes

music may fill the nights
intoxicate a troubled soul
it does not heal the
open wound

the streets of Havana
do not dance as easily
as they danced in my head

children are not postcards
they swarm for candy, for dollars
for whatever the hand opens to

old women retell their stories
sad prayers in broken
English
managing a word in Italian
in German any language
with a sympathetic ear

men peddle sin and cigars

*

there is no revolution
there are no revolutions
there is only humanity
the condition we are
there is only the need to

be
the revolution is
romance
it is Che in a black beret

*

i am a little ashamed
at my quest
for Hemingway's seat
where he rested and wrote
thinking a cigarette and beer
will comfort the moment
and history will give it
meaning

*

the child improvises life
on a burning street of broken concrete
lifting an empty box of chocolates
feeling richer for having a package
of chewing gum or kleenex
contemplating its value, its possibility

the men are busy re-inventing parts
for dead cars
busy resurrecting their existence
more beautiful than before

between the beer and cigarettes
i pull out my pen
the one i take for granted
knowing it is there

when i must scribble words into thoughts
into poems

my pen so easily mislaid
replaced
it is my pen
that will immortalize me

i do not have enough pens
in my tourist bag
to give to the children
who beg for them
for pencils
for paper
so they too
may write themselves out
of the moment
out of reality

how beautiful
how sad

Spanish Steps

i remember flowers in 1976
large pots
colours lining the stairs
as far up as the church
of *Trinità di Monti*
maybe i have imagined them
maybe i have wished them
they are not here now

only bodies
and more bodies
young bodies
women, men, hunters
of tender flesh
peddlers of romance

the sun flirts with everyone
regardless of age or size
it teases equally
and we are in love with
the playground

i remember thinking Keats
must have sat here
sat on the very same steps
his young frail body
needing the sun

he must have scribbled
words and thoughts
in a diary
so he would never
forget this place

Piazza Navona

i dine alone
it is a habit
my husband works nights

i dine alone
in Piazza Navona
it is a sin

the waiter is extra attentive
has taken pity on me
a woman alone in Rome
is a sorrowful sight

i, a woman of a certain age
beneath a Roman Spring
night sky

a half moon dangling over my head
bright as the flirtatious stars

i dine on *matriciana* and veal
a glass of red wine
my eyes on the gifts of Bernini
my heart wants to plunge into
the fountain

i must act out the game
it is fun to pretend

the waiter's English
is less fine
than my Italian

by the end of the meal we are
as close as *due paesani*

arrivederci comes with a smile
a touching of hands
two tentative lips
on the alluring cheek
of the woman
who dines alone

This Necessary City

this necessary city kicks my soul around like a soccer
    ball
this city of well-looked-after-needs, of children with
    designer
clothes, warm shoes
this city of percentages and polls
neat little piles of garbage tied into plastic bags
plastic boxes, plastic cans
where does it all go

i know there is more hidden in its folds
in the lane ways and corners, much more than
is necessary
it does not inspire
this city is the need to realize some makeshift dream
created with the same need to belong and to be
this is a place to pretend
i am tired of the race of choice between the heart and
    the eyes
nowhere to stop in this necessary city
nowhere to feast
or to cry
to have the tears absorbed and understood
how can we nourish the nothing, the expanse of
    nothing
the non-beauty of it all

where to go to decapitate the noise
this operatic strangle in my throat
the ringing in my ears

kick me, kick me hard, send me flying
i want to be a soccer ball
i want to find my soul

Cimitero, Ceprano

between me and this stillness
there is another body
it walks without discomfort
prances about
light as the ghosts
i have come to visit
i imagine my spirit
as it leads me to the corners
where my relatives have been
at peace for a while
corners i cannot remember
but find without difficulty

i have come to respect the dead
i have come out of duty
to living family
to deliver small pots of flowers
and light candles
i have come to honour the dead
who live in my head
large and loud as ever

i sit, light a cigarette
listen to the birds
the cypress trees tall and strong
i feel timeless
i can see the little girl i was
running between tombstones
chasing lizards
beyond the gate
the river stretching forever

the dripping greens of summer
beneath a pure white burning sky

this is not a place where the dead are
it is where i come to remind myself
i am still alive
i put out the cigarette
say good-bye
i walk away
and never feel the earth beneath
my feet

Song for Saro

you called me Giannissima
as if my birth name
was not large enough
to embrace all i appeared to be
inside your eyes

i was just a girl
a girl ripe for heartache
just another girl
in the little black book
and the little black heart
of your roommate

i was the girl who listened
to your guitar
and understood the songs
you wailed out in dialect
a dialect your own lover
found primitive

but it was she
who lay next to you
and loved your primitive soul
it was she
who sent you to heaven
and back

until love became too confusing
and dialects began dying

another immigrant boy
rides the sky tonight
with a mouth full of poems
in search of paradise

Torch Song

Rosaria sings her songs
from somewhere so buried
so dark
sometimes only she can go

her three languages
share one orphaned soul
escaped from a seaside town
by the red-clay toes of Vesuvius

the Argentinian sun
passionate and unforgiving
dug blazing holes in the romance
of a young woman's heart

he kissed away the wounds
for just a little while
until his lips
became razor blades
leaving her open
a banquet of wounds
we feast upon
each Friday night
by the light of vanilla candles
the aroma of sizzling garlic
and an old accordion's sigh

Rosaria sings her songs
and a thousand miles away
i hear Argentina cry

A Night After the Rosary

i open my heart to you
i open it in prayer
in fear
in desire
in need
and in desperation

i open my heart to you
i invite you in

my heart has been open
from the first moment
of memory
from the moment
i was guaranteed
your divinity
your absoluteness
your omnipresence

now i wait
for the promise you made
to erase the darkness
and paint in the light

how will i know
how large the space must be
for you to enter

and how much light will it take?

Faith

she has buried the last one
her son was first
at thirty-six
some cancer she didn't understand
in the bones
then the liver
it was fast
her husband was next
she understood heart attack
made it more real
almost acceptable
and at forty-two
something popped in Lia's brain
and she was gone
ethereally
a sigh
silently

she has buried all three
and accepts being alone
insisting
God knows
what He is doing

Poetry as Prophet

For Rubin Alves, Brazilian Theologian

have i suffered enough
to hope

do i dare hope
do i dare not

what is real
what is imagined

that i am loved
or hated
persecuted or exalted
do i walk into the fantasy
and feel fulfilled

am i skeptical
or simply without discipline

a misplaced desire
an immediate orgasm

i command the pencil
to move
scratch out creative symbols
in need of redemption

the need to exist
the courage to envision
poetry is the prophet
i am the fool

Some Priests

i have noticed
certain priests live well
are well versed
in many things
prepared for the argument
on the subject of their own
on the defense of their own

they have written books on
Augustine, Aquinas,
Francis, Peter and Paul

certain priests live their lives
among the finest books
among the masters in
the halls of wisdom
among the great painters
philosophers and kings

some priests never venture
out into the world

in *Piazza del Popolo*
there is a church
it is home to
Caravaggio's Crucifixion of Peter
and Conversion of Paul
it is home to the works of
Pinturicchio, Raffaele, Bernini
and many more

Padre Antonio
is a charming man
educated
skilled in psychology

he walks with me
and intimately explains this
beautiful church
the artists he has researched
are part of him
he speaks of them as if they
were residents
members of the parish

after the tour
i am honoured to eat with the brothers
a woman is welcome
but clearly out of place
i am temporary

when i leave
i am filled with food
with history and art
with the charm of the
Augustinian brothers
the beauty of a Roman church

but it is reality i walk into
it is the woman on the steps of
the church
the child in her arms

her hand
scarred
open
beneath the
cool shadow
of history

Perché ti amo

They keep taking each other to the sun,
they find they can easily

Ted Hughes

tu sei il sole di mezzogiorno
on my flesh
on a July afternoon
beneath the poplars
overlooking Georgian Bay
you are the cotton sheets
cool on my skin
the sweet taste of tonic
with lime and gin
your arms are what i fall into
i travel the length of you
with an appetite
the solid
fragrant island that you are
splendid
my island

The Student

the English words stumble out
of his boyish lips
the vowels rolling around
his tongue
trying to master all the sounds
the syllables
waiting for the music of the words
he reads the poetry
transcribes each image
his smile reassures me
the experience is pleasant
his questions are wise
like his eyes
one moment of enlightenment
and he thanks me
one moment and i am rich
for understanding

Marzo 21, 2003

forty-one years away
this spring day in my
birth town
in this peninsula of dreams
and memories
this peninsula loved by so many
princes, paupers and fascists

i am another immigrant
you have heard it all before
another torn and broken soul
forever in a storm
two moons
two hearts
two deaths

today is San Benedetto
the first day of spring
the birds are perched
on the railing lining the river
i sit by the statue of Padre Pio
fresh daffodils and mimosa
in a plastic vase

i look up at my cousin's building
in the town square
it is washed with the morning sun
her crisp laundry hanging from the balcony
the flag of peace
bright in its stripes of purple and yellow

the Bar Cavour crowded
with gentlemen who no longer
need to be anywhere at a
specific time
they drink coffee, linger
talk of war
of Iraq and Iran
of Saddam, Bush
and America
America
America
still the elusive America
like a song from their lips
no mention of Canada

you come from America
they ask
i answer
no
i come from here
America is where i live

i walk the tight winding streets
recalling the games
the skipping of cobblestones
savouring the smells from
open windows
the songs on the radio
the faces of old women
heavy bodies on straw chairs
their hands still busy

i let the sun walk with me
it keeps me warm

i shall leave this town soon
return to where i live
always a little bit fatter
a little bit sadder

Angels

For Maria Grazia

everywhere i hear talk of angels
angels of flesh
angels of stone
guardian angels
spirit angels
little fat baby angels

the Archangel
angels with wings
and those who walk among us
unnoticed

Maria Grazia lives with angels
high above the *piazza*
facing the church of Sant'Arduino

her angels are quiet
they sleep on her dresser
next to dry petals of flowers
scattered in a porcelain bowl

the winged ones hang on pale
sunburned walls next to her
mother's photographs

always the perfume of roses in the air
the flicker of candlelight

the bells of the church ring in each hour
the angels flutter their wings
they dance to the music

each time she enters the room
the angels smile
they know they are home

The Girls at Hotel Tre Stelle

they are excited
new ducklings in a
brand new world
all of them sixteen
pure
blood, bone, flesh
they are innocence
and incessant energy
their laughter defies acoustics
it slams into the room
shaking foundations
theirs is a playground of *fantasia*
they fear nothing
see only the magic
at sixteen
the magic is beautiful
it is all possible
it is all they need

such joy
watching my daughter's happiness
wanting it for her
endless
sharing it quietly in my heart
her friends
have so much more
of her now
their world so large
so hopeful
each moment an adventure
in breathing

laugh children
laugh out loud
your sounds explode
you are the
symphony

The Married Man

you appear in my life
a mysterious blemish

a tiny dark mole
not unpleasant
imbedded in my skin
i carry you with me
frivolous as you are
i do not think of you
until my eyes
fall on your irregularity
and when i see you
i cannot help but smile

His Wife

his wife greets me
with gentility

she is so much more
the elegance i lack

so much more the
sophistication of breeding
in colonized cultures of
money made and invested well

i am the gypsy girl
his mother feared
a maker of philters

the peasant girl with
contaminated blood

not worthy of a
mother's son . . .

he and i are a
short story unfinished
the invisible ink
the missing page
the steamy sequence before
the orgasm

Dead Woman at the Window

death comes calling
and i am sitting at the window
contemplating the world
outside my walls
my cats busy
in their daily affair
my plants quenched of thirst
from their morning drink
the photographs dusted
my mirrors free of streaks

my eyes are open
and my back resting
against the feather pillow
with the lace trimming
my hair neatly curled
by the pink sponge curlers
i bought at the dollar store
my blue fingers bent
over the one royal crown
coffee cup i have left

a day or two shall pass
and the voiceless cry
of my beloved cats shall
reach an ear

death comes so uninvited
so shameful and quiet

i shall rest my hands
on this favourite chair

and wait
until my friends begin to wonder
why i missed the bridge game

they will find me in this position
by the window
my faithful cats
licking my legs

how sad and tragic
they will say

death comes alone
without the multitude
of children
and grandchildren
without the noise of love

death comes
on a quiet day in spring
as i sit and watch the world
and my cats watch me

this is fine
this is just
fine

Costantino's Garden

on Applefield Drive
in the Scarborough wasteland
the garden is unattended
a few plants entrenched
to the ground
the ones he had tended to
waiting for May to co-operate
it was cold that millennium year
wet and cold
too unpleasant to dig up the soil
to plant the delicate shoots
much too early for the tomatoes

the grapevine is strong
older than he even remembered
planted when my cousins were
in short pants and played
hockey on the street
the grapevine will survive the
grandchildren and more

the pear tree is perfect
this autumn it will curve
easily with the weight of the fruit

the beans will not clamber
the wooden trellis
and the fragrance of basil will not
escape from the kitchen window
only the spade will lean by the shed
where the garlic hung white and fat
braided into pungent bouquets

the wheelbarrow retired
the garage door shut
only the memory
a fallen body
the quick finger snap of
a stroke
a blood clot
silent and respectful
my uncle's garden will sleep
in dreams of purple and red
absorbing the sweet, sticky
tears of the concord grapes
he loved

A Man Named Pete

my uncle Pete
worked in a quarry
by the cemetery
in my home town
somewhere between
Naples and Rome

he worked with great
slabs of stone
marble, granite
carved the names of
dead relatives and *paesani*
on the cool, smooth surface

sometimes he practiced
his art
he carved grand angels
and roses beside the names

when i was seven he shaped
a little granite goat with the name
Nella on its rump
it was my pet goat
that had survived
the Easter table
for two years
the third was unlucky
i kept that little granite goat
until i left my town for good

there is something in the way
you deliver your words

the way your body moves
in and out of circumstances
the way your face holds its history
without apology
it brings back my uncle

there is something real
about a man named Pete

In the End, Bonita

i have searched for clever words
to induce the laughter
laughter is the tonic we need
coats the pain
we have used the tonic often
over the years
to erase the mark left by both
students and administration
we have used laughter to explain
the unexplainable
when the words *fuck it*
might
have been appropriate

we have used the tonic best
among us
when the banquet was
a glass of wine, a cigarette
a naked heart

you understand the smile
we have shared that much
to make it here
still whole
with so much grace

they can keep their gold watch

Something Brand New

my father and sister
never sat in the same chair
never sat next to each other
on the sofa
ate at different times
tonight is so strange
their feet almost in conversation
as he holds her baby boy
and makes grandfather sounds
and she
is not his daughter
but somebody's mother
and tonight
they understand
each other

Analyze

i stumble
from emotion
to emotion
a blind woman
in a storm
i have never
been able to dissect
neither poem
nor frog

Romance of Fools

we have filled the room
with curiosity
ex-lovers
neglected friends
intellectuals
and would-be poets

we are here for you
Lazarus
for your resurrection
your re-incarnation

we believe in redemption
the possibility of transformation
but your tongue is still
sharp
your heart still bruised

our journey is
a romance of fools
claiming each time
a new love
a real love

the beginning

we are too much
the apple of ego

God and love
always get in the way

On a Country Road

the sky promises sunshine
you and i
in my blue honda
driving towards it
breaking off pieces
for our pockets

sitting beside you
i know your breathing
i know i am home

my mouth opens
there are things
i could interrupt
you with
but they will wait

this moment is
for my heart
pushing its way
into my eyes
beating
    burning

at the sight of you

Falling

falling apart
blame it on time
indulged habits
the price of aging
not reason enough
to embrace the lumps
inside the breast
the cancer in the liver
the burning and bleeding
womb

the brain crashes
we are each other's pillow
absorbing the blow
the tears

courage
instead of prayers
God doesn't always
intervene
He set it in motion
and must sit back
watch the outcome

we are the passive ones
we are the bullies

Void

how weak i am
when the day has
beaten me

how spineless
everything is too much
a challenge

i have lost my appetite
for confrontation
but my mouth swallows

like a shark
anything to fill the
empty space
i have eaten another
box of chocolates

Bella

Per Sophia

the English poet once wrote

truth is beauty
beauty is truth

that i shall search for this
all my life
to understand the meaning
of the words
simple as they are

if it should live in a smile
that unburdens the ordinary day
and makes it lighter to carry

if it should be in the colour of her skin
the earth offering the scent
of spring lilies fresh from the rain
if i should find it in her walk
the gentle movement of her hips

in her eyes that tell a story you believe
completely
as you watch her hands stretch
over the blanket, removing the creases
till the bed is an altar you cherish

and when you sit in her presence
in comfort, without the need to go
and attend to other things

when you look at her
and your heart says

è bella, è veramente bella

you know she is real
it is the truth of *her*
you discover

The Women I Am

i have grown large with the women
i am
heavy with passions and needs

mirrors inhabit my faces
each one different
each with something i recognize
my grandmother's eyes
my mother's nose
my sister's smile
each voice demanding to be heard
each heart craving a love of its own

i am a woman invaded
too many bodies to please
to attend to

i make you cry
but your tears are no longer moved
by my beauty
the radiance of my skin
the length of my hair
your tears are encouraged
by the other woman i am
the woman of anger
whose desires are much
too great for you to provide
she lives in the heart of regret
of dreams not met
of places not visited
this is the woman who hides
deep in the pocket of a full moon

i make you laugh
and it is another woman still
the one you caressed on
a summer night
in the month of August
foolish heart wanting laughter
promising youth
and love
forever

reckless dreamer living
between words and punctuation
beneath linens in hope chests
in flower pots and photographs

you love me
and i am the best of women
i am soft
free of pain
my face without lines
my lips red and inviting
i am moist
i am what you want to hold
what you need to secure who you are
the woman you wish
would always be home
i walk out
to divide the minutes of the day
the hours and the weeks
that swell into years
i come back with shadows

i linger
the smoke

of a smoldering fire
i am the memory of warmth
and light
a safe place
a room with curtains and soft chairs
Modigliani prints on a johnny-cake wall
long necked women with heavy heads
and thin eyes

so many women
so many appetites
lessening
drying
like blood drops
that will disappear
bleached away by the heat of the sun

Too Much

we are too much
the dream
we cannot live up to

too much
the children who should
have turned out right

we are too much
the breath of fantastic things
the innocence
in a space of lies

there is only this place
without celebration
the day
with all its demands
ordinary
untidy
there is only work to do
before and after the light
when we lie
on our mattress of relief
the solitude is
overwhelming

Cuore

my heart is a shovel
like my hands
it digs and turns over
each new season
new attempts at life

my heart is a seed
beginning again and again
the roots protected

my heart is a virgin
in a red dress
dancing into her
lover's arms

my heart is the poison
absorbed in small doses
the sadness indulged
by hormones

my heart is a dream
being wronged
too often

my heart is a coward
left with its mouth
wide open

Vita

it is about living the moment
not writing it
about the taste left on the tongue
the itch in the eye
it is about being there
collecting the shard
cleaning up the mess
reclaiming the position
writing is only
second best
it is about giving without
the necessary papers
slicing the mystery
deciphering the desire
it is the flesh combusting
the heart shifting
the necessary evil
the prayer

it is about ripening
tart
sweet
and feeding the hunger

The Perfume

For Gigi

the air is perfumed
with women

young women
shopping for love

old women
recalling the romance

pubescent girls
anticipating

their skin
intoxicates the air

this season
is the scent of women

this season is the kiss
on the breast

it is the mouth
open in desire
it is the one tanned leg
exposed

summer is the lover
that brings all things back

to the nostril
to the heart

The Dandelion

For Karen

the first dandelion
has bravely shaken
its bright yellow head
in your abandoned garden

i watch it stretch toward the sun
from my porch window
high above the aging cherry
it is the twenty second spring
in my house
it would have been the sixteenth
in yours

i am continually amazed
at the rebirth
terrified that each winter
will slice the roots forever
and it is the end

but the dandelion persists
it brings back my grandmother
in her bright cotton scarves
the sharp little knife in her hand
digging out the deep tentacles
shaking off the soil
filling the sack
with our evening meal

i think where you might have been
when i helped grandma dress the
green jagged leaves with oil and vinegar

were you tying their golden heads together
a yellow bouquet for your grandmother

two lifetimes beneath two far away moons
half a century
and we are just two women
who have watched a garden grow
two women who have loved
each other's children
tending their games
watching them take shape

how enchanting
the view
how amazing
a tiny
bitter weed

What I Miss

it is the landscape i miss
it is the unbelievable beauty
of a mimosa in bloom
of a fig tree with its ripe
sensuous fruit

it is the market on Saturday
the red tomatoes
the goat cheese salty and sharp
the birds on the windowsill
it is the smell of extinguished
wax candles at evening mass

it is about the way your skin feels
when it is awakened by memory
by the scent of something you
thought you had forgotten

it is Bernini's magnificent statues
washed in endless fountains
their glorious heads, arms
legs, breasts,
every corner of their perfection
free to love

it is the sun
that bathes our elegance
allowing us to parade our
egos in endless promenades
romantic fools that we are

going home is not impossible
it is too expensive
i have learned to live frugally
with memories and memorabilia

there is such a distance
between a young girl's dreams
and an old woman's prayers

the accumulation of dust
and tumours
hair falling and growing
in the wrong places
mirrors hung in the space of
windows

it is beauty i miss and
the tall umbrella pines
it is as simple as that

Sempre

he looks at me
they are the same eyes
watching my hand
pass the brush
through my wet
less opulent dark hair
shaking my head
to loosen the curls

on the second floor balcony
of the Auberge Charobois
my overgrown mass against
a white wall in a building
pretending to be Spanish

he speaks and his voice
still carries the slight accent
of his New Zealand roots

how many times have i watched
you comb your hair
on hot summer evenings
against a white wall

he takes me back
to the Villa Rosa
in Siracusa
to the white Sicilian sand
to wine sweet as vermouth
to prickly pears on cactus plants

he takes me back to the small
rented house carved into a hill
in Piemonte
back to Robin's terrace
overlooking Oriental Bay

the brush moves easily
through my thoughts

he has loved me perfectly
for so long
even the loss of my hair
does not disturb him

Maggie/Peggie

i dream i am Margaret Atwood
not a nightmare at all

i love my new silhouette
my small feet in penny loafers
pallid, clear skin
my Canadian skin
my Canadian heart
beating to a less chaotic drum

no more Neapolitan songs
weeping and tragic
no more De Sica and Magnani
this small immigrant life
this woman unknown

gone is my life in black and white
the black of death
mourning ancestors through
reminiscence and longing
the white of an unfamiliar landscape
indifferent and cold

no more misunderstanding identity
letting the passion loose
a mortal sin
devouring the language of too many vowels
where names are unpronounceable
unreadable

the displacement is gone
the loss
the numbness of invisibility

i am Margaret

i love my manicured hands
delicate
the perfection of my smile
the clarity of my name
the gentle
perfectly audible
perfectly edible
voice

Ceprano/Carnevale

tomorrow
the Lenten season
begins
forty days of renewal
and sacrifice
a time to dust off the
soul
revive the heart

it is *carnevale* and
this town is ready to party

i stand back and watch
the *piazza* ignite
costumes, music, laughter
children's limitless cries

i am a tourist now
in this town i once called home
this place i keep coming back to
looking for whatever it is
i might have left behind

it is not *my* town anymore
home is not about material
it is not the cobblestones
or the *piazza*
it is not the church or the
bells
although the umbrella pines and
the cypress trees by the cemetery
always felt like home

the bridge over the river
seems less impressive
there is the sour smell of centuries
in the walls of abandoned buildings
the stains and rubble left unattended

my grandfather's house sold
long before my
return
but the March sun is hot
on my face
i watch the children
dance in the town square
oblivious to time or history
it is all real and unreal

the old men and women
uncomfortable with age
leaning, holding on to arms
searching for empty benches
to rest the remaining bones
their eyes sometime land
on my lumbering presence
and i wonder if somewhere
in their memory they might
recognize the child i once was

the one who belonged here

but it is not home
that i come back to
i am simply a stray cat
bewitched by
curiosity

Invisible

i am sitting
once again facing the Stazione Termini
once again beneath the cool of the
palm tree
sipping the juice of sicilian oranges
the cigarette
the book
the brand new city map

the English couple at the next table
deep in conversation, their
matching pierced noses and brows
their purple and blue hair
replacing the *afros* and bleached
reds of my generation

i am back
here again, dowsed in traffic
in fumes, noise and splendour
here again for whatever it is
i am looking for

i am the invisible woman

not young enough to desire
not old enough to direct

i am middle aged
i walk and sit among the crowds
a weightless spirit
my l00 kilos unnoticed
my large breasts unimportant

Fellini would have loved me
Fellini should have loved me

but
it is the manicured nail of time
i now feel
precisely scratching out
any thought of romance from
my aging heart

i am now free

to stop in the gardens
to read the Latin words
on church walls
to notice how loud birds
are in the middle of March

i am now free

to walk with the stray mutt
who accompanies me to the
gates of the *camposanto*
then turns away
knowing he is not yet ready
for this *ultima passeggiata*

i can still see my face
in the young women
clustered in *piazze*
their freshness and anticipation
young bodies aflutter
new butterflies ready to
take in the sweet

to fly
to begin the joyous

i walk to the spaces i have been before
to the fountains and monuments
where i had promised to return
once again the ritual of coins
and wishes

this city is a mosaic of
scattered hearts
multicoloured petals on cobblestones
trampled with time
well worn into the ground
so many pieces
brilliant in the sunshine
it is difficult to recognize
the scraps that are mine

Ritorno

i have come back to the house
where i was born
but it is only the road i recognize
long, winding beneath the bridge
it is the smell of new grass
and the yellow mimosa in late March
that welcome me

the oak tree is gone
flattened into a driveway
the faded walls of a small house
revived by a bright melon
yellow
no more rosemary bushes
or grapevine

my cousin's wife is polite
she offers me coffee
in porcelain cups

we sit beneath her new
covered verandah
the red clay *canali* patterned
into waves
there is insignificant
chatter between us
we are strangers
she is in her fortieth year
and pregnant with her
third child
i am here unaccompanied

she escorts me to the bedroom
where i was born
i walk in alone
to an old woman
propped in a bed
a loud television
keeping her company

i move towards her
my feet arguing each step
her curious gaze suggests
she is aware
i must be a relative

ciao, zia

i tell her my name
she remembers
i am her
dead brother's child

she offers her hand
it is small
it has returned to the past
as all things do

Ti trovo bene

Sì, sì vedo che stai bene

i agree
i am well

i bring her Canadian chocolates
caramel sweet
she has no teeth
i am a little ashamed
at my arrogance
my ignorance

this irrelevant room
where my life
began
was once home

this room where my aunt
lies
solitary and toothless
waiting to go home